The Healing Corner

God is so intentional.

Be kind or be quiet.

Taylor Reames
Coaching and Consulting

"She speaks with wisdom,
and faithful instruction
is on her tongue."
Proverbs 31:26

40 Days to Heal the Heart You Don't Talk About

Angie Taylor Reames

The Healing Corner

Volume I

40 Days to Heal the Heart You Don't Talk About

Angie Taylor Reames

Copyright © 2026

Angie Taylor Reames

All rights reserved.

No part of this book may be reproduced, distributed, or transmitted in any form or by any means, including photocopying, recording, or other electronic or mechanical methods, without the prior written permission of the author, except in the case of brief quotations embodied in critical reviews and certain other noncommercial uses permitted by copyright law.

Scripture quotations are taken from the Holy Bible, New King James Version (NKJV), unless otherwise noted.

This book is a work of faith-based reflection and encouragement. It is not intended to replace professional medical, psychological, or counseling advice. Readers are encouraged to seek appropriate professional support when needed.

Printed in the United States of America.

Dedication

This book is dedicated to my family —
thank you for your patience, love, and support
while I healed from things
I never discussed.

To every person who has been hurt and needing to heal.
Thank you for allowing me the opportunity
to encourage you as you heal!

Table of Contents

Dedication 5

Introduction 9

DAY 1: Safe in His Arms 11
DAY 2: Permission to Feel 14
DAY 3: When Strength Becomes a Mask 17
DAY 4: Giving Yourself Grace 20
DAY 5: Naming What Hurt You 23
DAY 6: Healing Is a Process, Not a Moment 26
DAY 7: Rest Is Not Quitting 29
DAY 8: Letting Go Without Closure 32
DAY 9: When Forgiveness Feels Impossible 35
DAY 10: Healing Without Apologies 38
DAY 11: When Healing Feels Lonely 41
DAY 12: Releasing the Need to Be Understood 44
DAY 13: Healing Old Versions of Yourself 47
DAY 14: When Triggers Reveal Unhealed Places 50
DAY 15: Choosing Healing Even When It's Hard 53
DAY 16: Learning to Trust Yourself Again 56
DAY 17: Healing Does Not Erase the Memory 59
DAY 18: Setting Boundaries Without Guilt 62
DAY 19: When Growth Creates Distance 65
DAY 20: Grieving What Could Have Been 68
DAY 21: Allowing Yourself to Be Seen 71
DAY 22: Healing Requires Honesty 74

DAY 23: Learning to Sit with Silence 77

DAY 24: When Healing Changes Your Prayers 80

DAY 25: Trusting God with What You Can't Control 83

DAY 26: Healing Is Not Linear 86

DAY 27: Rebuilding After Broken Trust 89

DAY 28: Learning to Receive, Not Just Give 92

DAY 29: Releasing the Pressure to Be Perfect 95

DAY 30: Trusting the God Who Restores 98

DAY 31: Embracing Who You Are Becoming 101

DAY 32: When Healing Requires Patience 104

DAY 33: Reclaiming Joy Without Guilt 107

DAY 34: Letting God Redefine Strength 110

DAY 35: Healing Your Inner Dialogue 113

DAY 36: Trusting God with Your Whole Story 116

DAY 37: Releasing the Fear of Relapse 119

DAY 38: Walking Forward Without Fear 122

DAY 39: Trusting the New You 125

DAY 40: Walking Forward Healed and Whole 128

Closing Blessing *131*

About the Author *132*

Introduction

There are wounds we learn how to live with before we ever learn how to heal. Pain we carry quietly. Emotions we manage silently. Strength we perform daily — even when our hearts are tired.

The Healing Corner was created for the places you don't talk about — not because they don't matter, but because you didn't always have the space, language, or permission to share them.

This book is not meant to rush you. It is an invitation to sit, breathe, and be honest. An invitation to acknowledge what has been hidden, ignored, or pushed aside in the name of survival.

Healing is not weakness.
Healing is obedience.
Healing is courage.

Here, you are allowed to slow down. You are allowed to reflect. You are allowed to feel. And most importantly, you are allowed to heal.

Each page is a gentle reminder that God sees what you carry, understands what you couldn't explain, and is faithful enough to meet you right where you are.

Welcome to the healing corner.

Day 1

Safe in His Arms

> ### Scripture
> "He who dwells in the secret place of the Most High Shall abide under the shadow of the Almighty." — **Psalm 91:1 (NKJV)**

There are moments in life when strength is not what we need most — shelter is. Times when the heart feels fragile, emotions feel heavy, and the weight of everything unspoken becomes overwhelming. In those moments, God does not demand performance; He offers protection.

The secret place mentioned in Scripture is not a hiding place of fear, but a covering of love. It is where we are reminded that we don't have to be strong all the time. We don't have to carry everything alone. We are invited to rest.

Healing begins when we allow ourselves to be held — by God's presence, by His peace, and by His promise to cover what we cannot fix on our own.

You are not weak for needing rest. You are wise for accepting it.

Prayer

Lord, thank You for being my safe place. When my heart feels overwhelmed and my emotions feel heavy, remind me that I am covered, protected, and deeply loved by You. Teach me to rest in Your presence without guilt or fear. Amen.

Reflection Questions

- Where do I feel the need to be "strong" when God is calling me to rest?

- What does safety in God's presence look like for me right now?

- What would it look like to dwell in the secret place today?

_____
_____
_____
_____
_____
_____
_____
_____
_____
_____
_____
_____

Day 2

Permission to Feel

Scripture

"The Lord is near to those who have a broken heart, And saves such as have a contrite spirit." — **Psalm 34:18 (NKJV)**

Devotional

Many of us learned early how to survive by silencing our emotions. We learned how to smile through pain, push through disappointment, and keep moving even when our hearts were hurting. Over time, feeling became something we avoided rather than honored.

But God never asked us to numb ourselves to survive. He invites us to bring our whole selves — including our brokenness — into His presence. Scripture reminds us that God draws near to the brokenhearted, not the composed, not the polished, not the emotionally guarded.

Healing requires honesty. It requires permission to feel what we have buried, ignored, or minimized. God is not intimidated by your emotions. He is not overwhelmed by your tears. He is present in them.

Today, allow yourself to feel without judgment. What you feel is not a failure — it is information. And God is near.

Prayer

Lord, help me give myself permission to feel what I have avoided for so long. Remind me that You are close to me, especially in moments of emotional honesty. Heal what I have buried and restore what I have silenced. Amen.

Reflection Questions

- What emotions have I been avoiding or suppressing?
- What am I afraid might surface if I allow myself to feel?
- How can I invite God into my emotional healing today?

_____

_____

_____

_____

_____

_____

_____

_____

_____

Day 3

When Strength Becomes a Mask

Scripture

"My grace is sufficient for you, for My strength is made perfect in weakness."
— 2 Corinthians 12:9 (NKJV)

Devotional

Strength is often praised, admired, and expected — especially from those who have learned how to endure. Over time, strength can quietly become a mask we wear to avoid appearing vulnerable, needy, or overwhelmed. We learn how to keep going, even when our hearts are tired.

But God never intended strength to mean silence. Scripture reminds us that His strength is made perfect not in our ability to hold everything together, but in our willingness to admit when we cannot.

There is no shame in weakness. There is no failure in needing help. God meets us most intimately when we stop pretending and allow Him to see the parts of us that are weary, fragile, and worn.

Today, consider whether strength has become a shield instead of a support. Healing often begins when we lay the mask down.

Prayer

Lord, help me release the pressure to always be strong. Teach me that weakness is not something to hide, but a place where Your grace can meet me fully. Give me the courage to be honest with You and with myself. Amen.

Reflection Questions

- In what ways have I used strength to hide my pain?

- What would it look like to remove the mask and be honest with God today?

- Where do I need to allow God's strength to replace my own?

_____
_____
_____
_____
_____
_____
_____
_____
_____

Day 4

Giving Yourself Grace

Scripture

"As far as the east is from the west,
So far has He removed our transgressions
from us." — **Psalm 103:12 (NKJV)**

Devotional

One of the hardest parts of healing is learning how to extend grace to ourselves. We often forgive others more easily than we forgive our own mistakes, missteps, and missed moments. We replay what we should have done differently and quietly punish ourselves for what we didn't know then.

But God's grace does not come with conditions or expiration dates. Scripture reminds us that when God forgives, He removes — completely and permanently. There is no revisiting, no shaming, no holding our past over our heads.

Healing requires releasing the belief that you must suffer to atone for what has already been forgiven. Grace invites you to lay down self-criticism and accept the freedom God has already offered.

Today, give yourself the same grace God has already given you.

Prayer

Lord, help me receive Your grace fully. Teach me to release guilt, shame, and self-blame that no longer belong to me. Remind me that what You have forgiven, I am not meant to keep carrying. Amen.

Reflection Questions

- What past mistake or regret am I still holding against myself?
- Why is it difficult for me to receive grace?
- What would it look like to walk in freedom today?

_____
_____
_____
_____
_____
_____
_____
_____
_____

Day 5

Naming What Hurt You

Scripture

"He heals the brokenhearted
And binds up their wounds."
— Psalm 147:3 (NKJV)

Devotional

Healing does not begin with pretending the pain wasn't real. It begins when we are willing to name what hurt us — without minimizing it, excusing it, or rushing past it. Many wounds linger not because God hasn't healed, but because we never allowed ourselves to acknowledge them.

God is gentle with our pain. He does not demand explanations or timelines. He simply invites honesty. Scripture assures us that God heals and binds, which means He cares enough to tend to what is exposed.

Naming the hurt is not dwelling in it. It is bringing it into the light where healing can begin. You don't dishonor your strength by admitting what wounded you. You honor your healing.

Today, allow yourself to tell the truth — even if only to God.

Prayer

Lord, give me the courage to name what hurt me without fear or shame. Help me trust that You can heal what I am willing to acknowledge. Bind the places in my heart that are still tender and aching. Amen.

Reflection Questions

- What pain have I avoided naming out loud?
- What am I afraid might happen if I acknowledge it?
- How can I invite God into this place of healing today?

Day 6

Healing Is a Process, Not a Moment

Scripture

"Being confident of this very thing, that He who has begun a good work in you will complete it until the day of Jesus Christ."
— Philippians 1:6 (NKJV)

Devotional

Many of us wish healing could happen in a single moment — one prayer, one breakthrough, one release. But healing is often a process that unfolds slowly, gently, and intentionally. God is not in a hurry, and He does not abandon what He begins.

Scripture reminds us that God is committed to the work He started in us. That includes the parts of our healing that feel incomplete, inconsistent, or unresolved. Progress may feel slow, but it is still progress.

Some days you will feel strong. Other days you may feel tender and unsure. Both are part of the process. Healing is not measured by speed; it is measured by faithfulness.

Today, trust the process. God is not finished with you yet.

Prayer

Lord, help me trust You in the process of healing. When I feel impatient or discouraged, remind me that You are still working in me. Give me grace for where I am and faith for where You are leading me. Amen.

Reflection Questions

- Where have I expected healing to happen too quickly?
- What progress can I acknowledge instead of dismissing today?
- How can I trust God more deeply in this process?

Day 7

Rest Is Not Quitting

Scripture

"Come to Me, all you who labor and are heavy laden, and I will give you rest."
— Matthew 11:28 (NKJV)

Devotional

Rest is often misunderstood. Many of us were taught that rest means stopping, slowing down, or giving up. We learned to equate exhaustion with faithfulness and busyness with purpose. Over time, rest became something we felt guilty for instead of grateful toward.

But Jesus invites the weary, not the strong. He calls those who are tired, burdened, and overwhelmed to come and receive rest — not judgment. Rest is not quitting; it is responding to an invitation.

When you choose rest, you are not abandoning responsibility. You are honoring the limits God designed for you. Healing requires moments of pause where your soul can breathe and your heart can be restored.

Today, allow yourself to rest without guilt. Rest is not a setback — it is part of the healing journey.

Prayer

Lord, help me release the belief that rest equals failure. Teach me to receive rest as a gift from You. Restore my strength, renew my spirit, and quiet my heart in Your presence. Amen.

Reflection Questions

- What beliefs do I have about rest that may not align with God's truth?

- Where am I feeling weary right now?

- How can I intentionally accept rest today without guilt?

Day 8

Letting Go Without Closure

Scripture

"Trust in the Lord with all your heart,
And lean not on your own understanding."
— Proverbs 3:5 (NKJV)

Devotional

Not every wound comes with an explanation. Some relationships end without apology. Some seasons close without clarity. Waiting for closure can keep us tied to pain longer than God ever intended.

Letting go without closure requires trust — not in the situation, but in God. Trust that He sees what you never received answers for. Trust that He understands what was never acknowledged. Trust that He can heal what was never explained.

Closure is not always something we receive from people. Sometimes it is something we choose — by releasing the need to understand and placing our confidence in God's wisdom instead.

Today, consider whether holding on to unanswered questions is delaying your healing. God can bring peace even when explanations never come.

Prayer

Lord, help me trust You with what I don't understand. Give me the courage to release the need for closure and rest in Your truth. Heal the places that never received answers and fill them with Your peace. Amen.

Reflection Questions

- What situation am I still waiting for closure from?
- How has the need for understanding kept me tied to pain?
- What would it look like to trust God with unanswered questions today?

_____
_____
_____
_____
_____
_____
_____
_____
_____
_____

Day 9

When Forgiveness Feels Impossible

Scripture

"Be kind to one another, tenderhearted, forgiving one another, even as God in Christ forgave you." — **Ephesians 4:32 (NKJV)**

Devotional

Forgiveness is often one of the most misunderstood aspects of healing. We are told to forgive, but rarely taught how — especially when the wound is deep and the pain feels unresolved. Forgiveness can feel impossible when the hurt still feels close.

Forgiveness does not excuse what happened, nor does it deny the pain you experienced. It is not reconciliation, and it does not always require restored access. Forgiveness is a decision to release the burden of carrying resentment so your heart can heal.

God does not rush forgiveness. He invites us into it gently, reminding us that forgiveness is as much for our healing as it is an act of obedience. Sometimes forgiveness begins as a willingness — not a feeling.

Today, allow yourself to take one honest step toward forgiveness, even if that step is simply asking God for help.

Prayer

Lord, help me forgive where forgiveness feels difficult. Heal the places in my heart that are still tender and resistant. Give me the grace to release what I was never meant to carry. Amen.

Reflection Questions

- Who or what am I struggling to forgive?
- What fears surface when I think about forgiveness?
- What would one small step toward forgiveness look like today?

Day 10

Healing Without Apologies

Scripture

"But you, O Lord, are a God full of compassion, and gracious, Long-suffering and abundant in mercy and truth." — **Psalm 86:15 (NKJV)**

Devotional

Many people feel the need to explain or apologize for their healing. We apologize for setting boundaries, for choosing peace, for saying no, and for stepping away from what once hurt us. Healing can make others uncomfortable, especially when they benefited from our silence.

But healing does not require permission. It does not need justification or explanation. God's compassion is not conditional, and neither is the healing He offers. Scripture reminds us that God is abundant in mercy, not scarcity.

You are allowed to heal without apologizing. You are allowed to choose peace without defending it. You are allowed to grow beyond what once confined you.

Today, release the need to explain your healing journey. God understands it fully.

Prayer

Lord, help me walk confidently in the healing You are doing in me. Teach me to release the need to explain or apologize for choosing peace. Cover my heart with Your compassion and truth as I continue this journey. Amen.

Reflection Questions

- In what ways have I apologized for my healing or growth?
- Who am I afraid might be uncomfortable with my healing?
- What would it look like to choose peace confidently today?

_____
_____
_____
_____
_____
_____
_____
_____
_____
_____

Day 11

When Healing Feels Lonely

Scripture

"When my father and my mother forsake me,
Then the Lord will take care of me."
— Psalm 27:10 (NKJV)

Devotional

Healing can feel lonely, especially when the people who once walked closely with you no longer understand the journey you're on. Growth can create distance, and choosing wholeness can sometimes cost familiarity.

But loneliness does not mean abandonment. Scripture reminds us that even when human support shifts or fades, God remains constant. He draws nearer when others pull away. He stays present when conversations change and paths diverge.

Feeling alone does not mean you are doing something wrong. Often, it means you are doing something brave. God is with you in the quiet spaces, strengthening you for what's ahead.

Today, remember that you are never truly alone. God walks with you through every step of healing.

Prayer

Lord, comfort me in moments when healing feels lonely. Remind me that Your presence is steady and faithful, even when others do not understand my journey. Strengthen my heart and renew my trust in You. Amen.

Reflection Questions

- Where have I felt alone in my healing journey?
- How has God shown up for me in quiet or unexpected ways?
- What would it look like to trust God more deeply in this season?

Day 12

Releasing the Need to Be Understood

Scripture

"For My thoughts are not your thoughts,
Nor are your ways My ways," says the Lord
— Isaiah 55:8 (NKJV)

Devotional

One of the quiet burdens many of us carry is the desire to be understood. We want others to see our intentions, recognize our growth, and acknowledge our pain. When understanding doesn't come, we can feel unseen or dismissed.

But healing does not require validation from everyone. God understands the parts of your journey that others never will. He sees the internal shifts, the prayers whispered in private, and the strength it took to choose healing over familiarity.

Releasing the need to be understood frees your heart from unnecessary weight. It allows you to move forward without waiting for approval or explanation. God's understanding is sufficient, even when others remain confused.

Today, consider what it would feel like to rest in God's understanding instead of seeking it from people.

Prayer

Lord, help me release the need to be understood by everyone. Remind me that You see me fully and know my heart completely. Give me peace in trusting Your perspective over human opinions. Amen.

Reflection Questions

- Where have I been seeking understanding from people instead of God?

- How has the desire to be understood slowed my healing?

- What would it look like to rest in God's understanding today?

_____

_____

_____

_____

_____

_____

_____

Day 13

Healing Old Versions of Yourself

Scripture

"Therefore, if anyone is in Christ, he is a new creation; old things have passed away; behold, all things have become new."
— 2 Corinthians 5:17 (NKJV)

Devotional

Healing is not only about releasing what others did to us; it is also about making peace with who we were when we didn't know better. Old versions of ourselves often carry shame, regret, and self-judgment for choices made in survival mode.

God does not hold your past against you. Scripture reminds us that in Christ, old things pass away — not to be revisited or condemned, but to be redeemed. Growth means honoring who you were while embracing who you are becoming.

You do not need to punish your past self to prove you've grown. Healing allows you to look back with compassion instead of criticism. The version of you that survived did the best they could with what they had.

Today, extend grace to the person you once were. They carried you this far.

Prayer

Lord, help me release shame toward past versions of myself. Teach me to see my growth through Your eyes — with compassion and grace. Heal the places where regret still lingers and replace it with peace. Amen.

Reflection Questions

- What past version of myself do I still judge harshly?

- What survival choices did I make that deserve compassion instead of criticism?

- How can I honor my growth today without condemning my past?

_____
_____
_____
_____
_____
_____

Day 14

When Triggers Reveal Unhealed Places

Scripture

"Search me, O God, and know my heart;
Try me, and know my anxieties."
— Psalm 139:23 (NKJV)

Devotional

Triggers often catch us off guard. A comment, a memory, a tone, or a situation can stir emotions we thought we had already healed. When this happens, it's easy to feel frustrated with ourselves, wondering why something still affects us.

But triggers are not signs of failure — they are invitations to deeper healing. They reveal places in our hearts that still need attention, compassion, and care. God does not expose these areas to shame us; He reveals them so He can heal them.

Instead of resisting or suppressing what surfaces, allow yourself to observe it. Ask God what the trigger is revealing and what your heart still needs. Healing is layered, and God is patient with every layer.

Today, view triggers not as setbacks, but as signposts guiding you toward wholeness.

Prayer

Lord, help me respond to triggers with curiosity instead of condemnation. Show me what my heart is revealing and lead me gently into deeper healing. Thank You for being patient with me through every layer. Amen.

Reflection Questions

- What situations or interactions trigger strong emotional responses in me?

- What might these triggers be revealing about unhealed places in my heart?

- How can I invite God into these moments instead of resisting them?

_____
_____
_____
_____
_____

Day 15

Choosing Healing Even When It's Hard

Scripture

"I have set before you life and death, blessing and cursing; therefore choose life."
— Deuteronomy 30:19 (NKJV)

Devotional

Healing is not always the easier choice. Sometimes it feels simpler to remain familiar with pain than to step into the unknown territory of wholeness. Healing can require uncomfortable decisions, difficult boundaries, and honest self-reflection.

God invites us to choose life — even when that choice feels challenging. Choosing healing does not mean the journey will be painless, but it does mean it will be purposeful. Each step toward healing is an act of faith, even when emotions resist change.

There may be days when healing feels exhausting, slow, or inconvenient. On those days, remember that choosing healing is choosing yourself, your future, and the freedom God desires for you.

Today, recommit to the choice to heal — even when it's hard.

Prayer

Lord, give me the strength to choose healing when it feels difficult. Help me trust that Your way leads to life, even when the path feels unfamiliar. Guide my steps and renew my courage today. Amen.

Reflection Questions

- Where have I been tempted to choose familiarity over healing?
- What fears surface when I think about fully choosing healing?
- What is one intentional step toward healing I can take today?

_____

_____

_____

_____

_____

_____

_____

Day 16

Learning to Trust Yourself Again

Scripture

"For God has not given us a spirit of fear, but of power and of love and of a sound mind." — 2 Timothy 1:7 (NKJV)

Devotional

Pain has a way of shaking our confidence — not just in others, but in ourselves. After disappointment, betrayal, or prolonged hurt, we may begin to question our judgment, instincts, and decisions. Trusting ourselves can feel risky when past choices led to pain.

But God has equipped you with a sound mind. He has placed wisdom, discernment, and clarity within you. Healing includes learning to trust the growth that has taken place — the lessons learned, the boundaries formed, and the insight gained along the way.

You are not the same person you were when the pain first occurred. You have grown, prayed, reflected, and healed in ways you may not fully recognize yet. Trusting yourself again is not arrogance; it is acknowledging God's work in you.

Today, begin rebuilding trust with yourself — gently and intentionally.

Prayer

Lord, help me rebuild trust within myself. Remind me that You have given me wisdom, clarity, and discernment. Heal the places where fear has caused me to doubt my own judgment, and guide me forward with confidence. Amen.

Reflection Questions

- In what ways have past experiences caused me to doubt myself?
- Where do I see evidence of growth and wisdom in my life now?
- What would trusting myself again look like today?

_____
_____
_____
_____
_____
_____
_____
_____

Day 17

Healing Does Not Erase the Memory

Scripture

"Do not remember the former things,
Nor consider the things of old."
— Isaiah 43:18 (NKJV)

Devotional

Healing does not mean forgetting what happened. Some memories remain — not to torment us, but to remind us of how far we've come. Many people feel frustrated when healing doesn't erase the past completely, believing that remembering means they haven't healed.

But God never promised to remove memory — He promised to bring restoration. Scripture invites us not to live in the former things, not to be governed by them. Healing allows memory to lose its power. What once controlled you no longer defines you.

You can remember without reliving. You can recall without reopening wounds. Healing gives you the ability to look back without being pulled backward.

Today, allow yourself to release the pressure to forget. Healing is not amnesia — it is freedom.

Prayer

Lord, help me understand that healing does not require forgetting. Teach me to remember without pain and reflect without being bound. Restore my heart and renew my focus on what You are doing now. Amen.

Reflection Questions

- What memories still feel heavy for me?
- How have those memories changed as I've healed?
- What would it look like to remember without being controlled by the past?

_____
_____
_____
_____
_____
_____

Day 18

Setting Boundaries Without Guilt

Scripture

"Above all else, guard your heart,
for everything you do flows from it."
— Proverbs 4:23 (NKJV)

Devotional

For many of us, boundaries were never modeled as healthy. We were taught to be accommodating, available, and understanding — even at the expense of our own well-being. As a result, setting boundaries can stir guilt, fear, or the worry of disappointing others.

But boundaries are not walls meant to shut people out; they are guardrails designed to protect what is sacred. Scripture reminds us that guarding our hearts is wise, not selfish. Boundaries help preserve your peace, your healing, and your emotional health.

You do not owe anyone unlimited access to you. Saying no does not make you unkind. Creating distance does not mean you lack love. It means you are honoring the healing God is doing in you.

Today, release the guilt associated with boundaries. Protection is part of stewardship.

Prayer

Lord, help me set boundaries with wisdom and without guilt. Teach me to guard my heart in ways that honor You and protect the healing You are doing in me. Give me courage to say no when needed and peace in trusting You with the outcome. Amen.

Reflection Questions

- Where do I struggle to set boundaries out of guilt or fear?
- What boundaries might God be prompting me to establish?
- How can setting boundaries support my healing journey?

_____
_____
_____
_____
_____
_____
_____
_____
_____
_____
_____

Day 19

When Growth Creates Distance

Scripture

"Can two walk together, unless they are agreed?" — **Amos 3:3 (NKJV)**

Devotional

Growth often changes the way we move through relationships. As healing takes place, our values shift, our boundaries strengthen, and our tolerance for what once felt normal begins to fade. This change can create distance — not out of bitterness, but out of alignment.

Distance does not always mean disconnection is wrong. Sometimes it is simply the result of becoming healthier. Scripture reminds us that walking together requires agreement, and growth can reveal where agreement no longer exists.

It can be painful to acknowledge that not everyone can go where God is taking you. Releasing certain connections does not erase shared history or love — it honors the season that has passed and the healing that is unfolding.

Today, give yourself permission to grow, even if it changes who walks beside you.

Prayer

Lord, help me navigate the changes that come with growth. Give me peace when distance forms and wisdom to release relationships that no longer align with the healing You are doing in me. Guard my heart and guide my steps forward. Amen.

Reflection Questions

- How has my growth changed the way I relate to others?
- Where do I feel tension or distance as a result of healing?
- What relationships may God be asking me to hold differently?

_____
_____
_____
_____
_____
_____
_____

Day 20

Grieving What Could Have Been

Scripture

"Blessed are those who mourn,
For they shall be comforted."
— Matthew 5:4 (NKJV)

Devotional

Not all grief comes from loss we can name publicly. Some grief is quiet — mourning what could have been, what we hoped for, or what never materialized. These losses often go unacknowledged, leaving the heart to carry sorrow in silence.

God honors grief in all its forms. Scripture reminds us that mourning is not something to rush through or suppress. It is something God meets with comfort. Grieving what could have been does not mean you lack faith; it means you are human.

Healing includes allowing yourself to mourn unmet expectations and unfulfilled dreams. When grief is acknowledged, it creates space for comfort, clarity, and renewal.

Today, allow yourself to grieve without guilt. God is near to the mourning heart.

Prayer

Lord, comfort me as I grieve what could have been. Help me release unmet expectations and trust You with what lies ahead. Heal my heart with Your presence and fill the places of loss with Your peace. Amen.

Reflection Questions

- What expectations or hopes am I grieving quietly?
- How have I minimized my own grief?
- What would it look like to invite God into this grieving process?

_____

_____

_____

_____

_____

_____

_____

_____

_____

_____

Day 21

Allowing Yourself to Be Seen

Scripture

"The Lord does not see as man sees; for man looks at the outward appearance, but the Lord looks at the heart."
— 1 Samuel 16:7 (NKJV)

Devotional

Many of us learned how to be visible without being seen. We show up, serve, and function, yet keep the deepest parts of ourselves hidden. Being seen feels risky when past vulnerability led to misunderstanding, judgment, or hurt.

But God sees beyond performance. He looks at the heart — the intentions, the wounds, the quiet strength you carry. Healing invites us to consider whether we are willing to be seen not just by God, but by safe people He places in our lives.

Allowing yourself to be seen does not mean oversharing or losing discernment. It means choosing authenticity over isolation. Healing deepens when we no longer hide the parts of ourselves that need compassion.

Today, ask yourself where you may be hiding and whether God is inviting you into safe, honest connection.

Prayer

Lord, help me trust You with my vulnerability. Teach me how to be seen in ways that are healthy, wise, and healing. Surround me with people who can honor my heart and support the work You are doing in me. Amen.

Reflection Questions

- In what ways have I hidden parts of myself to avoid hurt?
- What fears surface when I think about being truly seen?
- Who feels like a safe person to share honestly with right now?

_____
_____
_____
_____
_____
_____
_____
_____

Day 22

Healing Requires Honesty

Scripture

"Behold, You desire truth in the inward parts, And in the hidden part You will make me to know wisdom." — **Psalm 51:6 (NKJV)**

Devotional

Healing cannot grow in places where honesty is avoided. Many of us learned how to manage pain without ever fully addressing it. We tell ourselves we are fine, that it doesn't matter anymore, or that we should be past it by now. Over time, those quiet denials can slow healing.

God desires truth — not perfection, not performance, not polished responses. He invites honesty in the inward parts, the places we don't often share with others. Healing begins when we stop editing our feelings and start telling the truth, first to God and then to ourselves.

Honesty may feel uncomfortable, but it creates space for wisdom and freedom. God meets us in truth, not pretense.

Today, allow yourself to be honest — without minimizing, excusing, or rushing past what you feel.

Prayer

Lord, help me be honest with You and with myself. Remove the fear that keeps me silent and give me the courage to face what I've been avoiding. Heal me with Your truth and lead me into freedom. Amen.

Reflection Questions

- Where have I avoided honesty with myself or God?
- What truths feel difficult to acknowledge right now?
- How might honesty open the door to deeper healing?

_____

_____

_____

_____

_____

_____

_____

_____

_____

_____

Day 23

Learning to Sit with Silence

Scripture
"Be still, and know that I am God."
— Psalm 46:10 (NKJV)

Devotional

Silence can feel uncomfortable, especially for those who have learned to stay busy to avoid what might surface. In silence, emotions rise, memories whisper, and truths we've avoided can finally be heard. For many, silence feels louder than noise.

But God often speaks most clearly in stillness. Scripture invites us to be still — not as a punishment, but as an opportunity to know Him more deeply. Silence creates space for awareness, reflection, and healing that noise can drown out.

Sitting with silence does not mean sitting alone. God is present there, offering peace, clarity, and gentle guidance. Healing deepens when we stop filling every moment and allow God to meet us in the quiet.

Today, practice stillness. Let silence become a place of connection rather than fear.

Prayer

Lord, help me be still before You. Quiet the noise around me and within me so I can hear Your voice clearly. Teach me to find peace in Your presence, even in silence. Amen.

Reflection Questions

- How do I usually respond to silence — avoidance or acceptance?
- What emotions surface when things become quiet?
- How can I intentionally create moments of stillness today?

_____
_____
_____
_____
_____
_____
_____
_____
_____
_____
_____

Day 24

When Healing Changes Your Prayers

Scripture

"Delight yourself also in the Lord, And He shall give you the desires of your heart."
— Psalm 37:4 (NKJV)

Devotional

As healing takes place, the way we pray often begins to change. What once felt urgent may now feel unnecessary. What we once begged for may no longer align with who we are becoming. Healing has a way of refining not just our hearts, but our desires.

God welcomes evolving prayers. Scripture reminds us that delighting in Him shapes the desires of our hearts. As we heal, we begin to ask not only for relief, but for wisdom, peace, and alignment with God's will.

Changed prayers are not a sign of weak faith — they are evidence of growth. Healing shifts our focus from simply wanting things to be different, to trusting God to make us whole.

Today, notice how your prayers may be changing. God is working in those shifts.

Prayer

Lord, thank You for meeting me in every season of prayer. As my heart heals, shape my desires to align with Your will. Teach me to trust You with what I ask and with what I release. Amen.

Reflection Questions

- How have my prayers changed as I've healed?

- What desires no longer feel necessary or urgent?

- How can I continue to align my prayers with God's will?

Day 25

Trusting God with What You Can't Control

Scripture

"Cast all your anxiety on Him because He cares for you." — 1 Peter 5:7 (NKJV)

Devotional

One of the hardest lessons in healing is accepting what we cannot control. We try to manage outcomes, fix people, and anticipate every possible scenario to protect ourselves from disappointment. Control can feel like safety, even when it quietly exhausts us.

God invites us to release what we were never meant to carry. Scripture reminds us that anxiety is not something we must manage alone — it is something we can cast onto God because He genuinely cares. Trust grows when we stop gripping tightly and begin surrendering daily.

Letting go does not mean you stop caring. It means you trust God enough to believe He is working even when you cannot see how. Healing deepens when surrender replaces striving.

Today, identify what you've been trying to control and offer it back to God.

Prayer

Lord, help me release what I cannot control. Teach me to trust You with my worries, my fears, and my unanswered questions. Remind me that You care deeply for me and are working on my behalf. Amen.

Reflection Questions

- What situations am I trying to control out of fear or anxiety?
- How has control affected my peace?
- What would surrender look like for me today?

_____
_____
_____
_____
_____
_____
_____
_____

Day 26

Healing Is Not Linear

Scripture

"For we walk by faith, not by sight."
— 2 Corinthians 5:7 (NKJV)

Devotional

Healing rarely follows a straight line. Some days you feel strong, clear, and hopeful. Other days old emotions resurface, and progress feels distant. When this happens, it's easy to believe you're going backward or failing at healing.

But healing is not measured by consistency of feeling — it is measured by faithfulness to the journey. Scripture reminds us that we walk by faith, not by what we see or feel in the moment. Fluctuations do not cancel progress; they reveal humanity.

God is present on strong days and tender ones. Moments of struggle do not erase growth — they often deepen it. Healing allows room for both progress and pauses.

Today, give yourself permission to heal imperfectly. God is walking with you through every step.

Prayer

Lord, help me trust You when healing feels uneven. Remind me that progress is still happening, even when I can't see it clearly. Give me grace for the process and peace in knowing You are with me every step of the way. Amen.

Reflection Questions

- Where have I judged my healing based on how I feel instead of how far I've come?

- What progress can I acknowledge today, even if it feels small?

- How can I extend myself grace in this season?

_____

_____

_____

_____

_____

_____

_____

_____

Day 27

Rebuilding After Broken Trust

Scripture

"The Lord is good to those who wait for Him,
To the soul who seeks Him."
— Lamentations 3:25 (NKJV)

Devotional

Broken trust can leave lasting wounds. Whether trust was damaged by betrayal, disappointment, or repeated hurt, rebuilding can feel overwhelming. Once trust is broken, guarding the heart can feel safer than risking vulnerability again.

God understands the impact of broken trust. He does not rush the rebuilding process or minimize the pain it caused. Scripture reminds us that God is good to those who wait and seek Him — even in seasons where trust feels fragile.

Rebuilding trust begins slowly. It starts with discernment, boundaries, and patience — not pressure. Healing does not require you to trust quickly; it invites you to trust wisely. God restores trust not by ignoring what happened, but by guiding you forward with care.

Today, allow yourself to rebuild at a pace that honors your healing.

Prayer

Lord, help me heal from broken trust. Give me wisdom to discern what is safe and patience to rebuild without fear or pressure. Restore my heart gently and guide me as I learn to trust again. Amen.

Reflection Questions

- Where has broken trust affected my ability to feel safe?
- What boundaries help protect my heart as I heal?
- How can I invite God into the process of rebuilding trust?

Day 28

Learning to Receive, Not Just Give

Scripture

"It is more blessed to give than to receive."
— Acts 20:35 (NKJV)

Devotional

Many of us are comfortable giving — our time, our energy, our care, our strength. Giving can feel familiar and safe, especially when receiving once led to disappointment or imbalance. Over time, however, constant giving without receiving can quietly drain the heart.

Scripture reminds us of the blessing found in giving, but it does not exclude the blessing of receiving. Healing includes learning how to receive love, support, rest, and care without guilt or suspicion. Receiving does not make you weak; it makes you human.

God often sends healing through others — through kindness, listening, and shared burden. When we resist receiving, we may unknowingly resist the very support God is providing.

Today, consider where God may be inviting you to receive instead of always giving.

Prayer

Lord, help me learn to receive with humility and trust. Remove any fear or guilt that keeps me from accepting the care You send through others. Teach me that receiving is part of the healing You desire for me. Amen.

Reflection Questions

- Why is receiving sometimes difficult for me?
- Where have I been giving without allowing myself to receive?
- How can I open my heart to receive support today?

_____
_____
_____
_____
_____
_____
_____
_____
_____

Day 29

Releasing the Pressure to Be Perfect

Scripture

"My grace is sufficient for you, for My strength is made perfect in weakness." — 2 Corinthians 12:9 (NKJV)

Devotional

Perfection often disguises itself as responsibility, excellence, or faithfulness. Many of us carry the quiet belief that we must get everything right to be worthy, accepted, or loved. Over time, that pressure becomes heavy and exhausting.

God never asked you to be perfect — He offered grace. Scripture reminds us that God's strength shows up most clearly where we are weak, not where we are flawless. Healing requires releasing the unrealistic expectations we place on ourselves.

Perfection can prevent rest, silence honesty, and delay healing. Grace creates room to breathe, grow, and be human. You are allowed to learn as you go. You are allowed to make mistakes and still be deeply loved.

Today, release the pressure to perform perfectly. God's grace is already sufficient.

Prayer

Lord, help me release the burden of perfection. Teach me to rest in Your grace instead of striving to meet unrealistic expectations. Heal the places where fear of failure has taken root and replace it with peace. Amen.

Reflection Questions

- Where do I place pressure on myself to be perfect?
- How has perfectionism affected my peace or healing?
- What would it look like to trust God's grace more fully today?

Day 30

Trusting the God Who Restores

Scripture

"And I will restore to you the years that the locust has eaten." — **Joel 2:25 (NKJV)**

Devotional

Some losses feel permanent. Time feels wasted. Opportunities seem missed. We look back and wonder what life might have been if pain hadn't interrupted the path we were on. Those thoughts can quietly steal hope if we're not careful.

But God is a restorer. Scripture reminds us that restoration is not limited by time, circumstance, or human failure. God is able to redeem what feels lost and bring purpose out of seasons that once felt empty or painful.

Restoration does not always look like getting back what was taken. Sometimes it looks like becoming someone wiser, stronger, and more grounded because of what you endured. God restores in ways that are deeper than replacement.

Today, trust the God who restores. Nothing you've been through has been wasted.

Prayer

Lord, help me trust You with what feels lost or delayed. Restore hope where disappointment has lived and bring purpose out of every season I've endured. Thank You for being faithful to redeem every part of my story. Amen.

Reflection Questions

- What seasons or years feel lost to me?
- How has God already brought growth or wisdom from those seasons?
- What would it look like to trust God with restoration today?

Day 31

Embracing Who You Are Becoming

Scripture

"Being confident of this very thing, that He who has begun a good work in you will complete it until the day of Jesus Christ."
— Philippians 1:6 (NKJV)

Devotional

Healing changes us. As the layers peel away and old wounds lose their grip, we may notice that we are no longer who we used to be — and that can feel both freeing and unfamiliar. Becoming someone new can bring excitement and uncertainty at the same time.

God is intentional in His work. Scripture reminds us that what He begins, He is faithful to complete. The changes you see in yourself are not accidental; they are evidence of growth, obedience, and healing in progress.

Embracing who you are becoming means letting go of expectations tied to old versions of yourself. It means allowing God to shape your future without clinging to who you once had to be to survive.

Today, welcome the person God is forming in you. You are growing into something beautiful.

Prayer

Lord, help me embrace who I am becoming. Give me peace as I release old versions of myself and courage to step into the growth You are producing in me. Continue the work You have begun, and guide me with Your wisdom. Amen.

Reflection Questions

- In what ways have I changed through this healing journey?
- What parts of my growth feel unfamiliar or uncomfortable?
- How can I trust God more fully with who I am becoming?

_____
_____
_____
_____
_____
_____
_____

Day 32

When Healing Requires Patience

Scripture

"But let patience have its perfect work, that you may be perfect and complete, lacking nothing." — **James 1:4 (NKJV)**

Devotional

Healing often teaches us patience in ways we didn't expect. We may feel ready to move on, yet our hearts still need time to process, settle, and strengthen. Waiting can feel frustrating when we're eager to feel whole and free.

But patience is not wasted time. Scripture reminds us that patience allows God's work to mature fully within us. Rushing healing can lead to unresolved pain resurfacing later. God's timing is intentional, even when it feels slow.

Patience creates space for depth. It allows healing to take root rather than remain surface-level. God is not delaying your healing — He is developing it.

Today, allow patience to partner with healing. Trust that God knows exactly what your heart needs.

Prayer

Lord, help me walk patiently through this healing journey. When I feel restless or discouraged, remind me that You are still working. Teach me to trust Your timing and rest in Your faithfulness. Amen.

Reflection Questions

- Where have I felt impatient with my healing process?
- What fears surface when healing feels slow?
- How can I practice patience with myself today?

_____
_____
_____
_____
_____
_____
_____
_____
_____
_____
_____

Day 33

Reclaiming Joy Without Guilt

Scripture
"The joy of the Lord is your strength."
— Nehemiah 8:10 (NKJV)

Devotional

For some, joy feels complicated. After loss, pain, or prolonged hardship, experiencing joy can bring unexpected guilt — as if happiness somehow dishonors what was endured. We may hesitate to laugh fully, celebrate freely, or feel light again.

But joy is not betrayal. Joy is restoration. Scripture reminds us that joy is strength, not denial. God does not heal us so we can remain burdened; He heals us so we can live fully again.

Joy does not erase what you've been through — it testifies to what God has brought you through. You are allowed to experience joy without explaining it, defending it, or apologizing for it.

Today, receive joy as a gift, not a contradiction to your healing.

Prayer

Lord, help me receive joy without guilt. Teach me that joy is part of the healing You desire for me. Restore my laughter, my lightness, and my ability to celebrate life again. Amen.

Reflection Questions

- Where have I held back joy out of guilt or fear?
- What moments of joy has God already restored to me?
- How can I intentionally welcome joy today?

Day 34

Letting God Redefine Strength

Scripture

"The Lord is my strength and my shield;
My heart trusted in Him, and I am helped."
— Psalm 28:7 (NKJV)

Devotional

For a long time, strength may have meant endurance — pushing through pain, staying silent, and holding everything together. While endurance has its place, God often invites us to a deeper understanding of strength.

Scripture shows us that true strength is rooted in trust. Strength is not just surviving; it is allowing God to help us. It is admitting when we need support and believing that receiving help does not diminish who we are.

God redefines strength as reliance, surrender, and trust. When we allow Him to be our strength, we no longer have to carry everything alone. Healing grows when we stop proving our strength and start resting in His.

Today, consider what strength looks like when God defines it — not pressure, but peace.

Prayer

Lord, redefine strength in my life. Help me trust You as my source and shield. Teach me to release the need to prove myself and receive the help You freely offer. Amen.

Reflection Questions

- How have I defined strength in the past?

- Where might God be inviting me to receive help instead of pushing through?

- What would trusting God as my strength look like today?

Day 35

Healing Your Inner Dialogue

Scripture

"Finally, brethren, whatever things are true, whatever things are noble, whatever things are just, whatever things are pure, whatever things are lovely, whatever things are of good report... meditate on these things."
— Philippians 4:8 (NKJV)

Devotional

Healing is not only about what happens around us — it is also about what happens within us. The words we speak to ourselves shape how we see our worth, our progress, and our future. Negative inner dialogue can quietly undermine healing, even when external circumstances improve.

God cares about our thought life. Scripture invites us to focus on what is true, noble, and life-giving. This does not mean denying hard realities; it means choosing not to dwell in self-criticism, shame, or fear.

Healing your inner dialogue takes practice. It involves noticing harmful patterns, interrupting them with truth, and extending compassion to yourself. God's voice is never condemning — it is corrective, loving, and hopeful.

Today, listen to how you speak to yourself. Healing includes learning to speak kindly within.

Prayer

Lord, help me become aware of my inner dialogue. Replace negative, critical thoughts with Your truth and grace. Teach me to speak to myself with the same compassion You extend to me. Amen.

Reflection Questions

- What patterns do I notice in the way I speak to myself?
- Which thoughts feel harmful rather than helpful?
- How can I intentionally replace negative thoughts with God's truth today?

_____
_____
_____
_____
_____
_____
_____

Day 36

Trusting God with Your Whole Story

Scripture

"And we know that all things work together for good to those who love God, to those who are the called according to His purpose." — **Romans 8:28 (NKJV)**

Devotional

It can be difficult to trust God with every part of our story — especially the chapters marked by pain, confusion, or regret. We may believe God works through the good, but hesitate to believe He can redeem what hurt us most.

Scripture reminds us that all things work together for good — not because everything is good, but because God is purposeful. Nothing in your story is wasted. Every experience, even the painful ones, can be woven into something meaningful.

Trusting God with your whole story means releasing the urge to edit or hide parts of it. Healing deepens when we believe God can bring beauty, wisdom, and purpose out of every chapter.

Today, consider what it would look like to trust God fully with your entire story — even the parts you struggle to understand.

Prayer

Lord, help me trust You with every part of my story. Remind me that nothing I've experienced is beyond Your ability to redeem. Give me peace in knowing You are working all things together for good. Amen.

Reflection Questions

- Which parts of my story do I find hardest to trust God with?
- How has God already brought growth or insight from past pain?
- What would it look like to surrender my whole story to Him today?

_____
_____
_____
_____
_____
_____
_____
_____
_____

Day 37

Releasing the Fear of Relapse

Scripture

"For God has not given us a spirit of fear, but of power and of love and of a sound mind." — 2 Timothy 1:7 (NKJV)

Devotional

After progress is made, a quiet fear can surface — the fear of going backward. We may worry that one hard day, one trigger, or one mistake will undo all the healing we've worked so hard for. That fear can cause us to tense up, overanalyze, or doubt our growth.

But God did not give us a spirit of fear. Healing is not so fragile that it shatters at the first sign of difficulty. Progress is built through consistency, grace, and God's sustaining presence. One difficult moment does not erase months of growth.

Relapse fears often signal a desire to protect healing — not a lack of it. Instead of fearing setbacks, we can trust that God equips us with power, love, and a sound mind to navigate challenges when they arise.

Today, release the fear of losing progress. Trust that God is with you not just in healing, but in maintaining it.

Prayer

Lord, help me release fear about going backward. Remind me that You have equipped me with strength, wisdom, and love to continue moving forward. Give me confidence in the healing You've already done and peace about what lies ahead. Amen.

Reflection Questions

- What fears do I have about losing the progress I've made?

- How has God already strengthened me to handle difficult moments?

- What would it look like to trust God with my continued healing today?

Day 38

Walking Forward Without Fear

Scripture

"For I know the plans I have for you," says the Lord, "plans to prosper you and not to harm you, plans to give you hope and a future."
— Jeremiah 29:11 (NKJV)

Devotional

Healing often brings clarity, and with clarity comes decision. As wounds heal, God begins to invite us forward — into new choices, new opportunities, and new seasons. Yet even with healing, fear can whisper reminders of past pain, urging caution and hesitation.

God's plans are rooted in hope, not harm. Scripture reminds us that the future God prepares is not designed to retraumatize you, but to restore and prosper you. Healing equips you to walk forward with discernment rather than fear.

Moving forward does not mean forgetting where you've been; it means trusting God with where you're going. The lessons learned through pain become wisdom that guides your steps, not chains that hold you back.

Today, choose to walk forward with hope. God's plans for you are good.

Prayer

Lord, help me walk forward without fear. Replace hesitation with hope and remind me that Your plans for my life are rooted in goodness and purpose. Give me courage to trust You as I step into what's next. Amen.

Reflection Questions

- Where do I feel hesitant about moving forward?
- How has healing prepared me for what's next?
- What would it look like to trust God with my future today?

Day 39

Trusting the New You

Scripture

"Do not be conformed to this world, but be transformed by the renewing of your mind."
— Romans 12:2 (NKJV)

Devotional

Healing often brings transformation that feels unfamiliar. As your mind is renewed and your heart becomes lighter, you may notice that your responses, desires, and boundaries have changed. The "new you" may not fit old expectations — including your own.

Transformation can feel uncomfortable because it requires release. Scripture reminds us that renewal begins in the mind, reshaping how we see ourselves, others, and the world around us. The new version of you is not a rejection of the past; it is the fruit of healing.

Trusting the new you means honoring growth instead of questioning it. It means believing that God knows exactly who He is shaping you to be.

You don't have to shrink to make others comfortable or return to old patterns to feel accepted.

Today, trust the transformation taking place within you. God is renewing you with purpose.

Prayer

Lord, help me trust the person You are shaping me into. Renew my mind and give me confidence to walk in the growth You are producing. Teach me to honor transformation instead of fearing it. Amen.

Reflection Questions

- In what ways have I noticed transformation in myself?
- Where have I doubted or questioned my growth?
- What would it look like to fully trust the "new me" God is forming?

_____
_____
_____
_____
_____
_____
_____
_____

Day 40

Walking Forward Healed and Whole

Scripture

"And the God of peace will crush Satan under your feet shortly. The grace of our Lord Jesus Christ be with you."
— Romans 16:20 (NKJV)

Devotional

Healing does not mean life will never be challenging again. It means you are no longer carrying yesterday's pain into tomorrow's purpose. You have learned how to pause, reflect, release, and trust God in deeper ways. That matters.

Wholeness is not perfection — it is alignment. It is knowing who you are, what you need, and where to turn when life feels heavy. God's peace now guards your heart with wisdom gained through experience and faith refined through healing.

As you step forward from this season, remember that healing is not something you complete and leave behind. It is something you carry with you — a way of living, responding, and trusting God day by day.

You are not who you once were. You are healed. You are whole. And you are prepared for what's next.

Prayer

God of peace, thank You for walking with me through this healing journey. Help me carry forward what I've learned and continue trusting You with my heart. Guide my steps, guard my peace, and strengthen me for the days ahead. Amen.

Reflection Questions

- What healing has taken place in me over these 40 days?
- How has my understanding of myself and God changed?
- What intentions do I want to carry forward into the next season?

Closing Blessing

May you continue to walk in healing long after these pages end.

May peace guard your heart and wisdom guide your steps.

May you trust God with what has been healed and what is still unfolding.

May you remember that healing is not a destination, but a way of living — rooted in truth, grace, and faith. And may you always return to God when your heart needs rest, clarity, or renewal.

You are not behind.

You are not broken.

You are becoming.

Amen.

About the Author

Angie Taylor Reames is an author, certified life coach, and ordained minister with a heart for healing, faith, and intentional living. Her calling is rooted in personal experience, shaped by pain, and refined through a deep desire to help others heal the parts of their hearts they often feel pressured to hide.

Angie became a certified life coach in 2016 and later answered the call to ministry, dedicating her life to walking alongside individuals navigating emotional healing, forgiveness, identity, and faith. Her work bridges practical life coaching with spiritual truth, offering compassionate guidance to both the churched and the unchurched.

She is the owner of Proverbs 31:26 Ministry, LLC and Taylor Reames Coaching and Consulting, LLC, where she provides faith-based coaching, mentoring, and resources designed to inspire growth, healing, and wholeness.

Angie is also the author of four additional inspirational works, including There Is Purpose in Your Pain, Perfect Imperfections – I Am Who I Am, and two prayer journals created to help readers deepen their connection with God through intentional reflection and prayer.

Through her writing, coaching, and ministry, Angie encourages others to heal honestly, love intentionally, and trust God through every season of becoming.

www.ingramcontent.com/pod-product-compliance
Lightning Source LLC
Chambersburg PA
CBHW030942090426
42737CB00007B/508